The Vastness of the Sky

Sheila Schofield Large

MOSAÏQUEPRESS

First published in 2022

MOSAÏQUE PRESS
Registered office:
70 Priory Road
Kenilworth, Warwickshire
CV8 1LQ

ISBN 978-1-906852-50-4

❖

For Pip

❖

Acknowledgements

'The Precipice, a short 16mm home movie', was first published on YorkMix Radio, 2020

'Part 4, in solidarity with Ian Dury', was first published by *The Poetry Kit*, 2022

❖

'Aedh Wishes for the Cloths of Heaven', by William Butler Yeats (1865-1939), first appeared in *The Wind Among the Reeds*, 1899

'Both Sides Now' by Joni Mitchell (b. 1943) was first recorded by Judy Collins in 1968, then appeared on the album *Clouds* by Joni Mitchell in 1969

'Remember', by Christina Rossetti (1830-1894), was first published in *Goblin Market and Other Poems*, 1862

'The Owl and the Pussy-Cat', by Edward Lear (1812-1888,) was first published in *Nonsense Songs, Stories, Botany and Alphabets*, 1871

Contents

Contents

❖

Had I the heavens' embroidered cloths,
Enwrought with golden and silver light,
The blue and the dim and the dark cloths
Of night and light and the half light,
I would spread the cloths under your feet:
But I, being poor, have only my dreams;
I have spread my dreams under your feet;
Tread softly because you tread on my dreams.

'Aedh Asks for the Cloths of Heaven'
William Butler Yeats

❖

❖

Life

Tears and fears and feeling proud
To say I love you *right out loud*
Dreams and schemes and circus crowds
I've looked at life that way

But now old friends are acting strange
They shake their heads, they say I've changed
Well something's lost, but something's gained
In living every day

'Both Sides Now'
Joni Michell

❖

Another slice of wedding cake

after Robert Graves

I wonder why other people's soap caresses
the skin like perfumed silk? Their virgin towels
hang perpendicular to the rail, or stacked
in a perfect pastel bale.

Log-burning halls welcome us with a soft inviting
light; not a thrown-off shoe or sock in sight.
A glimpse of sultry boudoirs hints at fine hi-jinks
in bed and Aga-infused kitchens exude Mary Berry's
lavender shortbread.

Do I always envy the lives of others
at the expense of my own?
Do I?
It might be so.

But the thing I so often wonder is why
other people's husbands so often have
a wandering eye?

Part 4 – in solidarity with Ian Dury

Our cue comes from the quick hit of your rhythm stick.
Timing that bumps along yet never misses. Forbidden
rhymes that strut about and spit impatience. Naked
and shameless. *Hammersmith Palais, Bolshoi Ballet,*
equal votes and porridge oats. We rocked and pogo-ed
to your poetry.

You honed the penetrating wit that fired out quips like
stones from slingshots. Cleaved your tortured path an
asymmetrical genius. Fought your corkscrew corner
with courage dressed as arrogance. Spasticus Autisticus
the battle-cry of difference.

We are your tribe. As one we rise. Our amputated limbs
would crawl the globe in several girdles. Blind, deaf and
mute we refute disabled labels. We are normal. It is they
who cripple us. We are Spasticus. We are legion. We are
one-eighth of their billions.

If the Earth turned on its axis to the rhythm of Spasticus
we would dance into infinity on two wheels. And if the
world were truly equal and acceptance universal, we'd
ride moonbeams, slide down starlight, we'd have
reasons to be cheerful.

Listen

It is a thing that defines me. My lip-synched
idiosyncrasy. Though it wasn't always so.

Lost decades of blaming bad diction, nodding
with conviction (often at the wrong question).

Nobody corrected me. Nobody told me that
the Four Tops did not sing If I were a carpenter

and you were a nail. Nobody else seemed at all
bothered that the Latin teacher's whispered falsetto

smothered every verbo so that I was given the lines
I must listen many times. Yet never got to know

my asinus from my cramped elbow. As time went on
quips became a useful quid pro quo for misfires.

(So Latin not entirely wasted - QED). Quintessentially,
living in a world of my own. But above all quiet.

Until the time came for help. Digital aid. The audiologist
was all smiles. Better? I nodded (with conviction) as

white noise battered around me. Traffic roared. Wildlife
chattered manically in the once hushed garden.

Then something called from above. A haunting cry
from childhood. A sound unnheard for so many years

as my damaged ears became more and more dull.
The mournful, magnificent call of a lone seagull.

Roman Holiday

after Juvenal (circa 1st to 2nd century CE)

These days satire is subdued. The news too bleakly
absurd to amuse. Who can credit a word in this world
turned arse-about-face against its own convoluted codes
of morality. Mortality is cheap. How easily we forget that
Empires expire. Rome stole democracy from Greece,
then twisted it to fit. The Senate itself a magnet for sadistic
endeavour. The Circus Maximus a forever doomed roar.
Whilst we are armchair voyeurs. Transfixed, as missiles
soar into another victim's war. Crushed limbs and stricken
faces out of place on our supersized sofas. An invasion of
our cosy reality. For levity we ogle the elite. Devour royal
antics. Hold street parties mired in nostalgic ire. Replete
with home-baked opiates; prosecco & poppy seed picnics.
We wave our arrogant passports as Hypnos leads us
sleepwalking through hoops of fire. And the ringmasters fiddle.
Lies drive a deadly bus through democracy. Soon it will be dead.
Yet we have our own grotesque circus.
Please pass the bread.

A Yorkshire lad

You'd be hard pressed to guess that lad's work. The mud
on his boots is not from a farm. He could be taken for a teacher,
I suppose, by his clothes and his general demeaner. Always

got a book under his arm. Has a clever look about him;
bit of a dreamer. Spends hours out in his shed I've heard,
though he's not a professional gardener.

The last one was more of a toff. Brought his young wife
to the old family 'ouse. Bitter and cold as the grave it was.
She didn't last long there, poor lass.

There's was another back in Victorian times, his motives
were mainly political. The first was eighteenth century, I think.
Man of the cloth. Bit too fond of the drink.

It's lonely here on the moor and the fell; they call to the poet
within us. Sometimes all that grandeur is hard to express,
we get ourselves tongue-tied - inarticulate.

It's as well we have yon lad on our side. Did you know
Yorkshire's had four poets laureate?

An equal moment

A snowflake lands on the back of your hand.
The symmetry in it's lattice thrills. Two atoms
of hydrogen astride one of oxygen start the slide;
the hexagonal dance of geometry. Six arms
in harmony. Six hexagons tesselate around six.
A perfect syntax of woven intricacy. Instinctively
you breathe that same oxygen deep into lungs
divided and divided again to the tiniest six of alveoli.
The mystery always in six. The smallest perfect number.
Carrier of karma. Nature's treasure. The beehive is a
storm of hexad construction; back to wax back combs of
sweet life. Hornets measure precise angles with antennae;
turn three-pronged Ys into nets of six-sided fortification.
The pattern expands. Stomps across the Giant's Causeway.
Dominates the winter sky. Six planets align. Join the dots.
Rigel, Aldebaran, Capella, Pollux, Procyon and Sirium:
a wonky hexagon. Inside, a straight line darts towards
Betelgeuse to form a perfect equilateral triangle.
And who can deny the vast symmetry of that?

No, we'll never tell them

Yesterday was hot. The air dust filled. The corn
high. Blood-red poppies nodded as they marched
in fine voice. Roses bloomed. Home fires burned.

Across a wide divide others also sang. Young and
fair, loud and cheerful. Lusty memories of
zuhause and the great good cause.

Tonight all advance in silence. Under a vast sky
pricked with stars. There is no moon. As the front
line draws close, a rose-tinted mist rises. A vision

creeps close. They have seen bad things, these boys.
Friends stumbling blind and terrified into fire; bloody
limbs flung aside and trodden black. But nothing

prepares them for this. These lads who walk on stout
legs, swing arms that hope to hold soft curves again,
lift up heads that should one day grow peacefully grey,

see only Hell as it stalks the valley of the Somme.
As one they stop. They stare. A breeze folds itself
around thin shoulders to whisper the truth of this

awful mission. They turn. Thousands. Hundreds of
thousands. More than a million young men march
back the way they came. The officers, bewildered,

fire into the fog as it swirls around their confusion.
Bereft of command, the pistol cracks cease
and a single lark soars through the clouds of peace.

Trapped waiting for Emergency Services...

The sky is true azure. Mid-way between
the old tower and the church spire is a large
tree; I believe an Indian Bean. They appear,

the tower and the spire, like medieval tyrants
in opposition. Poised in a celestial dance;
transcending the purely terrestrial.

I hear no sirens; only the tense hum of the
handful of onlookers and the rumble of
disembodied voices from an upstairs window.

Beyond the tree a small cloud rises. Violet as an
old bruise. Mine are new; indigo and ultramarine.
The sky is true azure, mid-way between.

Just a minute

Bored, I take a peek into mirror land.
You can lose yourself in there. It's a quite
different space. The furniture placed

with extra flair. The chair over by the fire
more inviting. The bookcase somehow more
profound. The reflected clock on the wall

shows the time at one minute past twelve.
A vase is spinning on the old round table
in the bay. Water pools in large, bright drops.

Yellow lilies lie gasping on the linen cloth
and pale voile curtains float in the breeze.
As I turn back into the room the same clock

chimes midday. The curtains billow into the room;
the vase tips and spins, lilies are strewn across the table.
Water drip, drip, drips on to the floor in bright drops.

Bored, you can lose yourself in mirror land.
For a minute.

Observation

It amuses me when at gatherings
of the chattering classes, on learning
I don't drink, people think
it's fair game to ask,
Is there a problem?

Whilst they, cheap chardonnay in hand,
can barely stand.

Self assessment

Is it a poisoned arrow in the flanks
of the working woman? An open
sore on the calloused hands of the
toiling man?

A constant thunderclap headache
for the wage slave mitigating debt.
An arthritic ache in the crumbling
bones of the old; that reflects a life
of much more give than get.

Or is it no more than a mere blemish
on pampered skin. A mild, rather
unpleasant, annual itch.

Is this what tax feels like,
to the rich?

❖

Loss

Remember me when I am gone away,
Gone far away into the silent land;
When you can no more hold me by the hand,
Nor I half turn to go yet turning stay.
Remember me when no more day by day
You tell me of our future that you plann'd:
Only remember me; you understand
It will be late to counsel then or pray.
Yet if you should forget me for a while
And afterwards remember, do not grieve:
For if the darkness and corruption leave
A vestige of the thoughts that once I had,
Better by far you should forget and smile
Than that you should remember and be sad.

'Remember'
Christina Rossetti

❖

Reflections on the vastness of the sky

for David Large 1922 - 2010

I have never seen a sky so wide.
It diminished me, that one. Truly diminished
everything. Stretched vast between two horizons.
Through wisps of cloud like wave-lapped sand,
I searched for your spirit beneath the infinite blue,
as we left behind that long straight road.
Seeming to float over cornfields on a low mist
that shifts through sunlight, the cathedral pinnacles
at Chartres, barely visible. Lost in a spiral of dust.
I journey, an unlikely pilgrim, through the labyrinth;
imagining your undulating breath then peace.
When we reach the coast I look to the heavens.
Suspended over a sea, dark as loss,
for no discernible reason there are fireworks.

For no discernible reason there are fireworks
suspended over a sea, dark as loss.
When we reach the coast I look to the heavens,
imagining your undulating breath then peace.
I journey, an unlikely pilgrim, through the labyrinth
at Chartres. Barely visible. Lost in a spiral of dust
that shifts through sunlight. The cathedral pinnacles
seeming to float over cornfields on a low mist
as we left behind that long straight road.
I searched for your spirit beneath the infinite blue,
through wisps of cloud like wave-lapped sand.
Everything stretched vast between two horizons.
It diminished me, that one. Truly diminished.
I have never seen a sky so wide.

The Precipice... a short 16mm home movie

Bavaria, 1939

He cuts a fine figure. Mein Herr.
Bolt upright against the granite craggs.
Squinting into winter sunlight. Not tall,
but somehow compelling. His bark
outsnaps my terrier. Testier
than his own vulpine hound.

In command of the Emperor's new sleigh,
he stalks blood-stained footprints across
icing-sugar snow. Devours strudel
with his Disney. *Sneewittchen* his favourite.
Snow White I am not. I am Gretyl. Chasing
happy-ever-after through dark woods.

He turns to share a narcissistic glare
with my camera. I beckon him to the left.
He ignores me. Thrusts an unforgiving boot
on to a ledge of ice-slicked scree.

His face is a picture. Mouth agape. Hands flailing
in futile salute. Arse over self-important tit.
Auf Wiedersehen. Gute Nacht.

I told him he was too far to the right.

Something to declare

1 – Rewind

The Union Flag rises over Brussels and flutters in a
new dawn. We care little for economic unity but can't wait
to take our little English lives over a channel afloat with hope;

choppy with opportunity. Our brightly striped espadrilles
barely brush Calais in the rush. Espadrilles. We taste the word
with thick coffee and toffee-apple tarts in village squares

where quick lizards hide in ancient stones. From sleepy trains
poppies flash through cornfields and a light-fingered mist lingers
on lime green hills. Like filings to the magnet of youth our band

expands. On dusty attic floors mattresses sigh with sleep
and the occasional whisper of amour. We earn an honest sous
serving foie gras and garlic snails on starched white linen.

Survive on ratatouille and rough red wine. In late bars looks
smoulder as we gather stoop shouldered over French tobacco.
The dark-eyed boy with the American lighter proffers Gitanes.

By day we lay on scorched sands. Supine. The brave among us
sublimely naked. The sloe-eyed boy continues to offer; blue smoke
ever calling to the gypsy in my soul. The gypsy who dances over

the drab past and catches a crystal-ball glimpse of the clasped hands
of unity. Holding a future that is safe in solidarity, rich with hope
and bright with the cloudless skies of summer.

II – Fast forward

The heart that once flipped at the flick of a Zippo
is now as dark blue as my new passport. The tatters
of the floundering flag lie at the feet of another continent.

Torn apart by the rent in the fabric of our future. St George
has slain the dragon and traded himself in poor sacrifice.
We are alone. A miserable little island mired in misplaced

nostalgia. Rigid with the dread of other. We have severed
the hands once held in ethnic brotherhood. Divorced
the sisters that share our turbulent history. Stripped naked

the fragile identity that shied from true unity. We turn
cold, lonely backs on the warm summer of youth to face
a world that shifts over uncharterted quicksand.

Perhaps I should have gone for the all-over tan. Said oui
to the Gitanes. Moved on with nothing left to regret. Now
I mourn those toffee-apple tarts. Our coffee is Americano.

Our espadrilles are uniformly black. Yet still we embrace our
neighbours in solidarity and a fragile hope that one day
they will take us back.

Small Game

It stands neglected now. The Weaver's House.
Though she did not weave. She wrote – which
is weaving of a sort. Ninety years old and so refined.

Woodsmoke wreathed over her roof and she hefted
in the logs herself. I wanted to call more often but was
put off by the horde of wild cats that she fed.

They'd stare. Arch-backed, yellow-eyed. Vicious.
They killed the blackbird's wife for fun. And once
when her kettle whistled out the back door a ginger

lunged, dagger-claws drawn, and scrawled blood down
my bare shins. One day there was no smoke. I ran uphill
through a scatter of tails. Battered at the door. Too late.

She was gone. Only the echo of a refined voice
played in my guilty head. *Keep them fed*.
It's the cats now who wreathe around my scarred legs.

They don't grieve. They hiss as they weave their hostile hex.
I could concoct a counter spell. Or leave them to take their chance
in hell.

At the edge of this world

Behind her clouds and land collide in a curtain
of weighted grey silk. Waves thrum on the shingle.
A black-winged wind sings. Out at sea she smells

frost smoke and something else. Blood; thicker than ice.
The moon casts a smooth white aisle over the ocean.
She might cross the path, touch the moon. Atone.

Cold penetrates her every bone. She will
wear no coat. His promise hangs over
them like a velvet key in calloused hands.

When he strokes the gloss of her hair he measures
its growth. At night she takes the sharp scissors and
clips it around her ears, small as seashells.

Her children thrive in this wild land. The boys strong,
fearless. Not one had flinched when she snipped
the webs between baby toes. Her daughter conflicted,

more easily shamed. Pained by the whispers -
Maighdeann-ròin. Selkie. She appears now through
frozen mist, her father's gift in reluctant arms.

She drapes the sliver skin around her mother.
Shrouded in its warmth, the woman turns and
dives headlong into the heave of the waves.

Moonlight, pale as loss, reflects on a seal-sleek head
and in the depths of the girls black eyes.

Legacy

High above an expanse of books is a wooden
box. Christmas cards – new. But for one,
a twinkly nativity. *Lots of love, Dad*.
My heart tugs tight.

Later an envelope thuds through the post.
A pack of Christmas cards painted by artists
without hands. They are delicate and deftly drawn.
My heart tugs again, though I'm not a fan of
this unsolicited marketing.

I catch sight of the sparkly Holy Family.
What would he have done? Dropping
the new cards into the wooden box, I reach,
deftly, for the cheque book.

Phobia

Vapour hangs in the morning air and shimmers over the
East River. Your head tilts to where the haze thins. Puffs
of cloud scud across the ribbon of blue between summits

that fall together: all but meet. A shudder follows
the sweat down your spine. You are five again. Grim
warehouses loom dark over docks that reek, at once

both sharp and dull, sweet and fetid. You scurry past
on short legs with no words to explain. Something knocking
to get out. Something locked away in the vault where monsters

shapeshift to fit the bogie man's shadow. Where unseen hands
set traps over fathomless holes. They are here now. Those hands.
Reaching in to claw and crawl like an ice caul around your heart.

You absorb yourself in the map. Delve into the axonometric city.
Monuments reduced to laminated blocks. Empire State, Flat Iron,
Chrysler. Liberty you left hovering on mist. The little ferry swaying

over waves of city debris. A jolly woman divined your aprehension.
Warned that inside you would climb a double helix to the crown
suspended over a gaping void to the feet. You block this image.

Erase it with the coffee froth of now. A street cleaner fills his lungs.
Oh sole mio! If you allow a smile will you fly? Up beyond skyscrapers;
beyond bogie-men; beyond the bad-dream remnant stalking you

on wind that tunnels between the geometric blocks. The scent
as powerful as those long-ago docks where demons played
and called to you on the salt-tang of the sea.

Consequences

In the bosky dapple of the woods
a memory creeps back, unbidden.
A summer nature walk; our random
task to find moss and lichen in the gloom.
We taste this new word under sulking trees,
roll it round our mouths. Reindeer food. Lichen.

At ten, the boys make enemies of lichen.
But for one, ungainly, yet at home in woods,
who scouts with girls through twisted trees.
Lends his birthday knife to all, unbidden,
and shrugs the kindness off like gloom
from his large frame. Our random

squad must win this test however random
the hunt. He will befriend the lichen;
find new moss, bright beneath the gloom
where only shadows bathe the woods
and yellow fungus grows unbidden.
Unstoppable, Lord of the Trees,

that dress themselves in fungus; the tree's
own bark well hidden. Champion of random,
who knew that he could lead unbidden;
that he would find his light through lichen?
Despite the creepiness in woods
that might dissolve children in its gloom.

Nineteen eighty-nine. History finds gloom.
A football crowd topples like felled trees.
Maybe he saw darkness; dappled woods,
(they say that memory in death is random).
Though nature can be born again in lichen,
a crushed heart cannot renew when bidden.

High commanders wrote the script unbidden
and cast around for guilt obscured by gloom.
They obfuscated stories in a veil, as lichen
forms to hide the natural bark of trees.
These leaders held their egos high in random
blame; seeing many trees but not the woods.

At ten he found that lichen blooms unbidden;
that moss, like boys, can blossom in the gloom.
But we all know that felling trees is never random.

*In memory of Patrick Thompson and
the other 96 killed at Hillsborough*

They promised the Earth

A proper winter, they forecast, with hoarfrost
on the hedgerow. Snow and berries, red
as madness.

But rain tsunamies through dank streets
where the slate sky hangs low enough
to touch; fingers no longer nipped with frost.

The dull grey segues through to spring. Not a single
snowdrop nor a lonely daffodil raises its head.
All are dead. The core of stored life rotted away.

As days lengthen the stifling sun does nothing
to alleviate the saturated mud. An acrid stench rises
from the awful swamp.

And autumn? Now I truly mourn. The word itself
woven with ochre mist and rich, fungal musk. Now
we trudge through rotten green and puce sludge

that follows us... like retribution.

When I know that we are way beyond the cautionary,
is the day the word *season* disappears altogether
from the dictionary.

❖

Love

They dined on mince, and slices of quince,
Which they ate with a runcible spoon;
And hand in hand, on the edge of the sand,
They danced by the light of the moon,
The moon,
The moon,
They danced by the light of the moon.

'The Owl and the Pussycat'
Edward Lear

❖

It was never about the lies

after Carlo Collodi

The road snakes ahead. Dusty. Hostile. Yet familiar.
Past the empty woodwork shop, sign askew. Through
the twisted orchard where we hid, upside-down
on skinny legs. Stole fat fruit and, once, the wig
from an old man's head.

On to the scruffy cafe where I sold my new school books.
Though they cost my father his winter coat.
I didn't ask for books. Or education.
I wanted freedom and adventure.

There was the cat... and the fox. Dad always knew.
Sad black eyes chastised my every lie. An old dad.
How he embarrassed me. Shabby poverty
worn like a tarnished badge.

He waits on the blistered porch with a jug of iced
lemonade and the warm caramel drift of my favourite
baked apricots. I hand my latest diploma into his smile.
He asks if I'm glad to be home. I breathe
oleander and jasmine. The drink bitter-sweet
in my city throat

where a sob breaks. My father,
who caught me in every juvenile lie,
also knows when I cannot deny
a reluctant truth.

Rose tinted

Something breaks your sleep. A creaky hinge.
A broken shutter. Shadows stutter across the face
of a huge full moon. Trace purple bruises through
a rose-pink hollow. Follow the ghostly patterns
on to red silk. Hanging. Expectant.

No white lace. No orange blossom. Only patchouli.
Musk masking the scent of youth. Mocking consent.
You are warm putty in hennaed hands. Faraway friends,
full of idle snapchatter, no longer matter. They will bloom
on summer streetcorners. Futures wide open under this
same ochre moon.

And tomorrow you will wait, sanguine. Breathe
rajnigandha and jasmine. Your future standing by.
Handsome, young, generous; worth the sacrifice?
Tonight beneath the Rose Moon with the bruised face,
you know that kind and gentle will suffice.

The universal soldier...

He folds his uniform with precision. Lays it on
a sandstone bluff high above the rough sea.
Places boots on top. The ceremony complete,
the wet prints of determined feet disappear
into the shock of waves. Behind him loom the
darkening dunes and a memory of virgin limbs.
Entwined. The act, for all the fuss, over in a flash.
Though nonetheless spectacular for that.
With the last stupendous shudder came peace.
The awful tremble in his hands stemmed. He knew
then that he would not go back. Could take no more
of the fear that claws at his heart like the rats that
gnaw on the unburied dead. The telegram will reveal
no detail. Missing. Presumed dead. A presumption
he can only hope will prevail, as he clambers now
over moss-slimed rock. Struggles with course cloth
on salt-wet skin. Breathes deep the unfamiliar musk
of sweat and sheep mingled with the bittersweet
juniper that creeps along the upward path.

Optimism

He said that her feelings were like glass.
Why then so careless? Why fragment them
into tiny useless shards? Pierce her heart
with a thousand needle-sharp barbs?

His smile is a crooked gash across the armour
of his steel face. Why indeed? Because
she offers a heart too fissile. Because
she invites destruction. Because
       to love is to present the glass half full
       Then wait for the crash.

The Viceroy's wife

after Vita Sackville-West

Hands have personalities; woven intricately with our own.
Drawing off shabby gloves, she observes hers now
with some detachment. Their marvellous articulations.

The bracelets of wrinkles encircling the wrists. The skin
pale and paper thin, with the dark speckle of a quail egg.
Despite a lifelong obedience to white gloves.

Her rings are burdensome. A great weight of rubies,
sapphires, diamonds. Tokens of his affection yes; but
no less the badges of embellishment proper to his rank.

Late-afternoon sun catches the largest gem. Refracted
colour plays across her hands. Once again they are
the ivory doves that melted in his viceregal clasp.

A shaft of light slants into the shop window. It raises fires
on the spent passion, the burnt out desires, of so many
disappointed rings.

Wednesday's Child

She is the ultimate altruist. Her virtues
worn openly on threadbare sleeves. Though
faith and hope are so often slapped back at her.
Charity stoned to death in the marketplace.
The curdled milk of human kindness flung
in her trusting face. No matter. She wipes it
away with a veil of compassion. There is no
motherhood for her. As though, growing inside,
benevolence has annexed all available space.
Until one grey Wednesday a shadow passes by
with a small child. War-torn and lost. Brooks no
argument. Gives her no choice. But places the
dusty hand into hers. She gazes at the boy.
Bewildered. Though somehow not surprised.
Call me mum she says, folding her son
forever in her goodness.

The knock

They meet in that secret place,
these three sisters-in-arms of peace.
Ears still ringing from the onslaught
of words that hurt every bit as much
as sticks and stones. At times the verbal
battering is worse. Now they huddle
together to rehearse what to do if discovered.
If old lives come knocking at the well-meaning
door of sanctuary.

One fears for her face.
Acid has been a frequent promise.
Another for her life. The slick flick of the knife.
The pitiless hands. Her slim, obedient neck.
The third holds a dead weight inside. Unable
to voice the awful truth. The terrifying conviction.
That if he were to arrive, indignation ablaze; anger
contained behind the iron face of coercion,
she would find a way
to return to him.

Wonder Woman

I've been working on the extension for some time.
It takes a lot of effort to create new and intricate
interiors. I am homemaker. Weaver of dreams.
Wonder woman.

I've been around a bit. Widowed more than once
I won't be tied down. This one only visits when he
feels frisky. Though he does travel a great distance
to see me.

But he's not the only one with a bit of frisk in them.
I contemplate the empty space on the black silk, licking
my laviscious lips.

Now if I was going to be a super hero
I would not choose the dubious lifestyle
of a male spider.

A question of colour

for Ashvin

He is a man of orange. And of red; thrilled by the scorch of
umber sands. The fires of sunset. He is unmoved by the
generic brown which become itself a race to those
who have no real interest in his culture. Brown

moves nothing within him. Unlike the scarlet elipses
of prickly coral; the vermillion of water lilies; the myriad reds
of the desert honeysuckle that scrambled over crimson
hibiscus in the lush of the garden at home.

Not for him the cool hues of the north. These he leaves to her.
She plants sky-blue ipomea to spiral up the cold face of English
brick. Creates a cobalt drift of bluebells at the feet of dark trees;
sows gentian, campanula, larkspur; scatters cornflowers to sway
through new wheat, the pale gold of her hair.

North and south. Opposites of the globe. Complements
on the colour wheel. When they swirl together an amethyst
jewel emerges. Violet as sunrise. Red-blue as blood. The purple
extracted from rare snail glands in ancient Tyre. Favoured by
Moses; demanded by Roman generals. The purpora of Homer;
the poetic footwear of Sappho.

These two will not be defined by simple colour. Neither brown
nor white portray anything of this celebration of difference.
Their mixing, which is more rare, more precious, than all
the riches of Tyrian purple.

*Recreating Tyrian purple dye required 12,000 rare, spiny-dyemurex snails
to make enough to dye a handkerchief.*

About the author

A poet, writer and tutor, Sheila reflects on the extraordinary in the every day and the small details in the bigger picture. She also sees humour in the face of pathos with hope usually emerging triumphant. She is driven by a love of language and inspired by respect for the power of words. Following an influential career in the UK social sector, Sheila now lives in south-west France where the pace of life and the wide-open spaces allow her to explore the ridiculous, the tragic and the pivotal lessons in life, loss and love. A lifelong pacifist, Sheila is influenced by a wide range of poets and writers from the classical to the modern, particularly those with a social message. Her work has been published in *Poetry News*, online by Yorkmix and The Poetry Kit and in numerous anthologies, and broadcast on radio in the UK and France. This is her second collection; it follows *Thin Ice*, which was published by Mosaïque Press in 2019.